Stand There!

She Shouted

Stand There!
She Shouted

THE INVINCIBLE PHOTOGRAPHER
Julia Margaret Cameron

SUSAN GOLDMAN RUBIN

ILLUSTRATED BY BAGRAM IBATOULLINE

CANDLEWICK PRESS

For "the most beautiful old" photographer,
Michael B. Rubin
S. G. R.

To Tatiana and her daughter Margo
B. I.

Text copyright © 2014 by Susan Goldman Rubin
Illustrations copyright © 2014 by Bagram Ibatoulline
Photography credits appear on pages 70–71.

First edition 2014

Library of Congress Catalog Card Number 2013953403
ISBN 978-0-7636-5753-6

14 15 16 17 18 19 CCP 10 9 8 7 6 5 4 3 2 1

Printed in Shenzhen, Guangdong, China

This book was typeset in Esprit.
The illustrations were done in acrylic gouache.

Candlewick Press
99 Dover Street
Somerville, Massachusetts 02144

visit us at www.candlewick.com

*It is a sacred blessing which has attended
my photography; it gives a pleasure to millions
and a deeper happiness to very many.*

—JULIA MARGARET CAMERON

*O*f all the girls in the Pattle family, Julia Margaret was the plain one. Her sisters, on the other hand, were known for their beauty and grace. People called them "the beautiful Miss Pattles." Except for Julia Margaret.

A woman who met her described her as "a little, ugly, underbred-looking thing; but she has the reputation of being very clever, which is better than beauty."

Julia Margaret didn't feel jealous of her sisters, though. She adored them, and they inspired in her a "deeply seated love of the beautiful." Years later, as a pioneer photographer, she *created* beauty with her camera. "I longed to arrest all beauty that came before me," she wrote.

She created *beauty with her camera.*

3

Julia Margaret spent her earliest years in Calcutta, India, where she had been born. At that time, 1815, India was part of the British Empire. Her father, James Pattle, an Englishman, worked for the British East India Company. The company had been formed mainly for trading spices, tea, cotton, and silk. James had joined the company at age seventeen as a "young gentleman writer," or clerk. Over the years in Calcutta, his positions grew in importance and he earned a small fortune.

The Pattle family lived in a big, comfortable house a few miles from the city, along the Hooghly River. A staff of Indian servants took care of them. Julia Margaret and her sisters played in a garden blooming with bougainvilleas, poinsettias, and sweet-smelling roses. Mynah birds and green parakeets flew through the air, and chattering monkeys swung from the trees. Water buffalo cooled off in the muddy river.

Growing up, the girls spoke Hindi as well as English and French. And for the rest of their lives, they spoke Hindi among themselves, especially when they wanted to have a private conversation.

The English colonials believed that the climate in India was not good for children. The hot, wet weather bred diseases such as malaria. During the monsoon season, the downpours brought epidemics of cholera. So the custom was to send children back to England for their health and education at age five or six.

Julia Margaret's mother decided to take her daughters to France to stay with her mother. Grandma l'Etang had moved from India to France two years before Julia Margaret was born. She had a house in the city of Versailles, as well as an apartment in Paris. When Julia Margaret was three years old, she boarded a ship bound for France with her mother; her six-year-old sister, Adeline; and her younger sister, Sara. Baby Maria was born along the way.

Leaving her father behind in Calcutta was hard for Julia Margaret. When would she see him again? She longed to have something to remember him by. . . .

English colonials believed that the climate in India was not good for children.

The long voyage around the coast of Africa took several months. To pass the time, passengers played cards, read books, or, in calm weather, fished for sharks. Julia Margaret and her older sister, Adeline, probably went exploring. On the deck stood crates holding live chickens and rabbits, and pens enclosing sheep and calves, waiting to be slaughtered for shipboard meals. During a storm, furniture flew across the cabins. The passengers ate their meals on the floor because cups and plates would have gone sliding off a table.

At last, Julia Margaret, her mother, her sisters, and the newborn baby arrived safely in France.

They stayed with Grandma l'Etang in Versailles at her four-story house opposite the cathedral, or, when they visited Paris, in Grandma's elegant apartment on rue de Provence.

After two years in France, Julia Margaret's mother returned to Calcutta without her daughters. Julia Margaret was only five years old. Parting from her mother was terrible. The painful separations from her parents deeply affected Julia Margaret and later inspired her to take and give photographs as keepsakes. They also made her closer to her sisters and grandma than to anyone else in the world.

For the next eleven years, Grandma l'Etang raised Julia Margaret, Adeline, Sara, and Maria. One day, their mother came back to visit and brought with her a new baby sister, Louisa. Then she left again for Calcutta, and over the next few years gave birth to Virginia, Harriet, and Sophia.

In Versailles, Julia Margaret and her sisters romped through the countryside unsupervised. The girls didn't go to school or have a tutor, because in those days, girls couldn't attend universities or enter professions.

Despite not having a formal education, Julia Margaret enjoyed Romantic poetry, Shakespeare's plays, and novels by popular authors. One of her favorite books was a French novel titled *Paul and Virginia*. The story told of a boy and a girl raised by two French women on an island in the Indian Ocean. The fatherless children come to a tragic end. Their plight touched Julia Margaret, who missed her own father. Many years later, she was to interpret the story with a photograph.

Julia Margaret and her sisters also read the Bible every day, said family prayers, and went to Sunday services, and she developed a strong religious faith. Looking back, she recalled wandering around Versailles and stopping in "dusty lanes" to kneel and pray when the beauty of nature overwhelmed her. Later she described her photographs as the "embodiment of a prayer." Images of the Virgin Mary fascinated her. Julia Margaret didn't realize it, but she was storing these pictures in her mind to use later in her art.

Many years later, she was to interpret the story with a photograph.

Grandma l'Etang taught Julia Margaret and her sisters the importance of good social skills. The girls learned how to run a large household of servants and how to host a party. In France, gatherings of high-society men and women were called salons. The emphasis was on good conversation.

The girls also took dancing and drawing lessons and studied piano. In the palace at Versailles, formerly the royal court, they viewed collections of art and fine furniture that had belonged to King Louis XIV. In Paris, they visited the Louvre Museum. There Julia Margaret thrilled at the work of the Old Masters, especially Raphael, and his paintings of angels and the Madonna. The pictures made a lasting impression on her, and later she directly borrowed some of their compositions for her photographs.

While in Paris, the girls most likely strolled through the gardens of the Tuileries Palace and fed the fish in the ponds. They may have stopped for ice cream at a fashionable café. Grandma l'Etang surely bought tickets for them to see the exciting new attraction at the Jardin des Plantes: a giraffe!

And they went to one of the many theaters and saw plays. Julia Margaret gained a lifelong love of theater and later often posed her models as though they were performing scenes.

During these years, Grandma l'Etang was grooming her granddaughters for one main purpose: marriage. In those days, the early 1800s, there were few career choices for women. Some became governesses or nurses. Others worked as seamstresses or shopkeepers. Even women with low-paying jobs gave them up when they married.

In 1830, when Julia Margaret was fifteen, her older sister, Adeline, left for England to meet a suitable husband. When Julia Margaret was eighteen, it was her turn. Grandma l'Etang had done her best to transform Julia Margaret into an attractive, poised young lady, but she was still short, squat, and strong willed. She was also lively and energetic.

In the summer of 1833, Julia Margaret met her father in London, where he had been on a home leave. It was the first time she had set foot in England in her life, although she considered herself an Englishwoman. With her father, she sailed back to Calcutta and joined the ranks of young women who were seeking husbands among the Englishmen employed by the British East India Company and the army.

Despite all that, her sister Sara was the one who married next, in 1835, then Maria, in 1837.

In May 1836, tragedy struck the family when Adeline died on a sea journey. Julia Margaret was heartbroken when she heard the news. Her grief made her physically sick with bronchitis and dizzy spells. So, as was the custom, she left Calcutta for the milder climate of Cape Town, South Africa, in October, to rest and regain her health.

During her stay, Julia Margaret became friends with Sir John Herschel, a noted astronomer. In addition to studying the stars, he experimented with the new invention of photography and was the first to use that word to describe it. For years scientists like Herschel had been trying to find a way to record images of people and places. On trips Herschel carried a device called a camera lucida. It was a drawing tool that enabled him to make precise drawings of scenes he viewed. But he wanted something mechanical that would create the picture for him.

In his experiments, he discovered hypo, a chemical solution that would fix images on paper and prevent them from fading in the light. Herschel shared his discovery with Louis Daguerre in France and William Fox Talbot in England. Both Daguerre and Talbot were racing to successfully invent the first camera.

Herschel must have told Julia Margaret about these exciting developments in photography. He knew that she took an interest in scientific matters. They formed a lasting bond, and he was to greatly influence her work. She later wrote to him, "You were my first Teacher & to you I owe all the first experiences & insights which were given to me."

Through Herschel, she met Charles Hay Cameron, a scholarly lawyer employed by the East India Civil Service. Cameron had been working in Calcutta to reform India's criminal laws. His health had broken down, and, like Julia Margaret, he had come to Cape Town to get well.

They began spending time together. Both of them enjoyed literature and discussing ideas. Although he was twenty years older than she, they were well suited. Soon they fell in love. When they sailed back to Calcutta together, they were engaged.

On February 1, 1838, Julia Margaret married Charles Hay Cameron. She was twenty-two; he was forty-two. From then on, she was known as Mrs. Cameron. Years later, when she took up photography, he was to be one of her favorite models, even though he giggled when posing. Once, when a visitor came to their house, she led the guest upstairs to peek at her sleeping husband and said, "Behold the most beautiful old man on earth!"

In Calcutta, the Camerons started a family that was to number six children. First, in December 1838, came a daughter named Julia, whom they called Juley. Then a son, Eugene, in 1840. Julia Margaret happily took care of her babies while running her household and hosting picnics and boating parties.

"Behold the most beautiful old man on earth!"

She corresponded with Sir John Herschel, who had returned to England. In her letters, she wrote of her "pure joy" as a mother. In his letters, Herschel told her about the latest advances in the field of photography. On January 6, 1839, Louis Daguerre had announced his invention of a camera that fixed an image onto a silver-coated copper plate. In that same year, William Fox Talbot published news of *his* camera, which used light-sensitive paper to make a negative.

In a letter to Julia Margaret dated 1842, Herschel enclosed two dozen talbotypes, or calotypes. These were small pictures made with the process invented by Talbot and were the first photographs Julia Margaret ever saw.

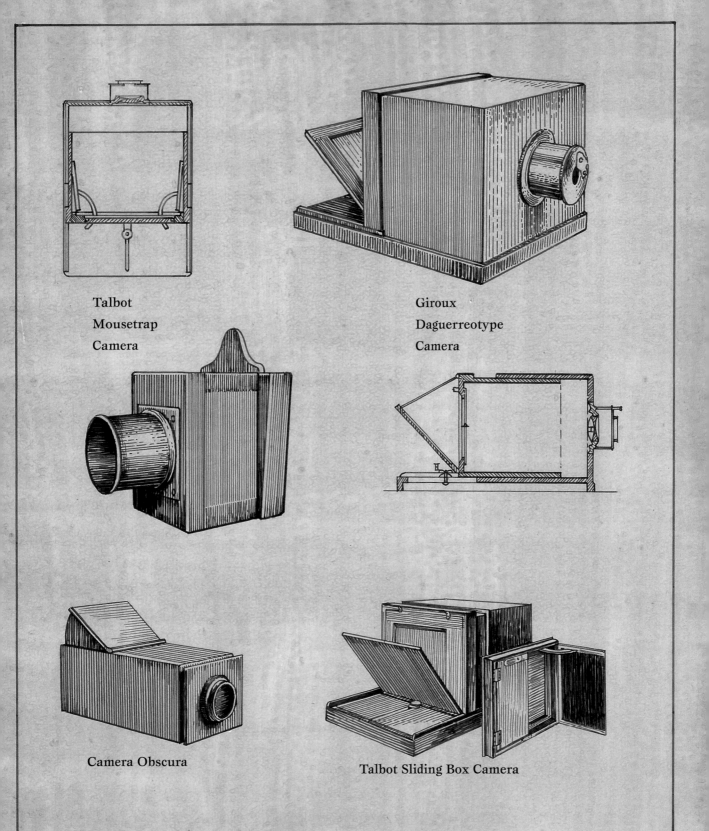

Talbot
Mousetrap
Camera

Giroux
Daguerreotype
Camera

Camera Obscura

Talbot Sliding Box Camera

For the next six years, the Camerons lived happily in Calcutta. Another son, Ewen, was born in 1843. Shortly afterward, they had to painfully part from Juley and Eugene, following the tradition that had separated Julia Margaret from her own parents. It wasn't long before the Camerons missed their older children so much that they decided to move to England after the birth of their fourth child, a son named Hardinge Hay.

On the way to England, they stopped in Ceylon, where Cameron owned estates that he planned to turn into coffee plantations. Ceylon, today called Sri Lanka, is an island in the Indian Ocean near the southern tip of India. To Cameron, it was paradise. But he and the family continued on to England and at last, in 1848, were reunited with Juley and Eugene.

Over the next few years, Julia Margaret gave birth to two more sons, Charles Hay Jr. and Henry Herschel Hay, named for her dear friend. Raising six children occupied most of her time. But some of her sisters had also moved back to England, and they visited back and forth.

Julia Margaret and her sister Sara had shared an enthusiasm for art and culture since their upbringing in France. They especially enjoyed the company of artists, writers, and musicians. Shamelessly they stalked celebrities and invited them to salons at Sara's home, Little Holland House. The gatherings took place every Sunday. The many distinguished guests included Alfred Tennyson, the Poet Laureate of England. Out on the rolling lawn, Tennyson read his poems "Maud" and *Idylls of the King* aloud, much to Julia Margaret's delight, and they became good friends.

At the salons, Julia Margaret also struck up friendships with a group of painters known as the Pre-Raphaelite Brotherhood, or P.R.B. for short. These artists admired the early Italian painters of the thirteenth century, who came before the Renaissance painter Raphael. The P.R.B. painted pictures of beautiful women with long flowing hair, and their work enchanted and inspired Julia Margaret. One of the members, George Frederic Watts, lived at Sara's house in exchange for teaching drawing to her children and sketching guests. He painted a portrait of Julia Margaret and made her a little more attractive than she actually was. Later, when she took up photography, Watts and Julia Margaret's sister Sophia posed for her in the garden at Little Holland House. Watts gave her tips about composing pictures. Many of her photographs of lovely women exactly duplicate the poses of the models in paintings by Watts and other members of the P.R.B., and she sometimes used Watts's model May Prinsep.

Many of her photographs of lovely women exactly duplicate the poses of the models in paintings.

Julia Margaret and her sisters were considered bohemians because of their arty friends and the way they dressed. They refused to conform to the stuffy Victorian standards of tightly laced corsets and stiff crinoline petticoats. The Pattle sisters draped themselves in loose gowns and Indian shawls and sported armfuls of bracelets that jangled as they walked.

An old friend of Julia Margaret's from her Paris days was the novelist William Makepeace Thackeray. He came for a visit in England and brought his daughter Annie with him. Annie later recalled her first impression of Julia Margaret as "a strange apparition in a flowing red velvet dress, although it was summer time." When the Thackerays left for the train station, wrote Annie, Julia Margaret came with them, "trailing draperies" and carrying a cup of tea, "which she stirred as she walked along."

Around this time, the 1850s, cameras became more readily available and sparked a sensation. Photography studios sprang up everywhere, and people clamored to have their portraits taken. The sitters dressed up in their best clothes and posed formally in front of a painted backdrop. The small portraits, called *cartes de visite,* measured 2 inches by 3½ inches and showed the figures in full length from head to toe. Queen Victoria, a model wife and mother, had photographs taken of herself; her husband, Prince Albert; and their children. Portraits of the royal family appeared on *cartes de visite* that were sold cheaply on street corners.

During the "cartomania craze," Julia Margaret visited a photography studio for the first time. She wanted a portrait of her oldest son, Eugene, who had joined the Royal Artillery and was about to leave. Having a picture of him before he "loses the look of peace!" she wrote, would help ease the awful pain of separation.

She grew interested in the new process and hired professional photographers to

She wanted a portrait of her oldest son, Eugene.

take pictures of her family and famous friends. Julia Margaret arranged the photos in albums and gave them as gifts. One of the photographs shows her youngest sons at her side. The picture is said to have been taken by an amateur, Charles Dodgson, also known as Lewis Carroll, the author of *Alice in Wonderland*.

By now Julia Margaret's daughter, Juley, had grown up and was married to Charles Norman. They had a baby girl, and Julia Margaret was overjoyed at the birth of her first grandchild. The baby, Charlotte, was born while Julia Margaret's husband was away in Ceylon.

During his absence, she visited her dear friends the Tennysons at their house, Farringford, in Freshwater, on the Isle of Wight. And she fell in love with the place. The Isle of Wight, an island off the south coast of England, has a milder climate than the rest of the country. It had become a popular holiday resort, especially when Queen Victoria built a summer house there. So in 1860, when Julia Margaret's husband came back to England, they leased two adjacent cottages in

Freshwater, next to Tennyson's home. Julia Margaret added a tower connecting the rose-covered cottages, and they named their home Dimbola Lodge after their estate in Ceylon.

When Cameron went to Ceylon again in 1863, Julia Margaret missed him so terribly that her daughter and son-in-law gave her something for Christmas to cheer her up: a camera and a darkroom kit.

Juley said, "It may amuse you, Mother, to try to photograph during your solitude at Freshwater."

Julia Margaret was intrigued. "The gift from those I loved so tenderly added more and more impulse to my deeply seated love of the beautiful," she wrote. To her, the camera was "a living thing," and, "unassisted," she learned how to use it.

"I began with no knowledge of the art," she wrote. "I did not know where to place my dark box, how to focus my sitter."

The "dark box" was a bulky wooden camera mounted on a tripod. The camera and tripod were so heavy that it took two men to move the equipment. Julia Margaret used the wet-plate process. This meant taking the picture with a glass plate negative, which she placed in back of the camera behind the lens. Each plate measured 9 inches by 11 inches and had to be coated with a chemical called an emulsion. If the cmulsion wasn't spread evenly, the picture would have streaks.

a. "dark box" camera with tripod
b. plate holder
c. emulsions
d. plate hand-buff
e. leveling stand
f. plate rack
g. sensitizing box

She converted her coal shed into a darkroom for developing the negatives. And she turned the chicken coop with windows and a glass roof into a studio. ("The hens were liberated," she wrote. "I hope and believe not eaten.") She called the studio her "glass house."

From the start, Julia Margaret wanted to portray subjects naturally and capture their inner selves as well as their outward appearances. For her, photography was an art form to express beauty and emotion. The first person who posed for her was a local farmer. But Julia Margaret spoiled the picture by rubbing the chemicals off the negative before she had a chance to print it.

"All thro' the severe month of January," she wrote, "I felt my way literally in the dark thro' endless failures."

At last, on January 29, 1864, she produced a photograph that she termed her "first success." The subject was a nine-year-old girl, Annie Philpot, who lived in Freshwater. Rather than showing Annie's whole figure, Julia Margaret had taken a close-up of her face and shoulders. Annie is lit

She produced a photograph that she termed her "first success."

by daylight shining through the glass roof of the chicken coop. Julia Margaret had covered certain panes with dark cloth and left others exposed to direct the light exactly where she wanted it, creating highlights and shadows. Julia Margaret was ecstatic with her results. "I ran all over the house to search for gifts for the child," she wrote. Then she framed the photo and sent it over to Annie's father with a note that read: "My first perfect success in the complete Photograph owing greatly to the docility & sweetness of my best & fairest little sitter."

Inspired by her accomplishment, Julia Margaret worked hard at her new career all winter. She took one lesson from photographer David Wilkie Wynfield, whose pictures she admired. Like Wynfield, Julia Margaret wanted to produce portraits that were more artistic than the cheap *cartes de visite*. Her goal was to create Art, with a capital *A*.

In a letter to her friend Sir John Herschel, she asked for technical advice. "I get into difficulties + I cannot see my way out of them," she wrote, and told him of accidents that caused failures. The accidents included scratches, chemical stains, prints turning green, and blurry images.

"My out-of-focus pictures were a fluke," wrote Julia Margaret. But the "fluke" pleased her artist's eye, and she began to purposely take pictures that were out of focus. The soft effect became her trademark.

The soft effect became her trademark.

She snagged all kinds of people to pose for her. Her husband, who had returned from Ceylon; their thirteen-year-old son, Henry Herschel; their maids; neighborhood children; nieces; nephews; her grandchildren; visiting friends. She even pursued strangers. "Why does not Mrs. Smith come to be photographed?" she asked about a woman in London whom she had never met. "I hear she is *Beautiful.* Bid her come and she shall be made *Immortal.*"

Tourists at Freshwater might be strolling along, gazing at the sea, when she boldly approached them. "I am Mrs. Cameron," she would say in a harsh voice. "Perhaps you have heard of me. You would oblige me very much if you would let me photograph you. Will you let me do so?"

Julia Margaret thought that posing for her was an honor and privilege. Her models, however, considered it an "ordeal."

"We came at her summons," recalled Annie Thackeray. "We trembled — or we should have trembled had we dared to do so — when the round black eye of the camera was turned upon us."

"It was torture *to sit so long."*

The studio (formerly the chicken coop) "was very untidy and very uncomfortable," recalled a woman who posed.

For a picture titled *Despair,* Julia Margaret locked her model in the studio for a couple of hours to get the right expression on her face.

Models had to hold completely still for ten minutes. "It was *torture* to sit so long," one of them said. Not to mention that Julia Margaret often dressed them in costumes to stage a scene.

"Mrs. Cameron put a crown on my head and posed me as the heroic queen," recalled a woman. "A minute went over and I felt as if I must scream; another minute, and the sensation was as if my eyes were coming out of my head; a third, and the back of my neck appeared to be affected with palsy; a fourth, and the crown which was too large began to slip down my forehead." So Julia Margaret started all over again and didn't stop until she had what she wanted.

The process of taking a picture involved first cleaning and polishing the glass plate. Next, she would coat the plate with a chemical solution called collodion and soak it in a bath. Then the plate had to be placed in a fixing solution, then washed and dried. And last, she applied a coat of varnish. The sitter had to hold still through all this as Julia Margaret scurried back and forth. She would throw away a hundred spoiled negatives before getting a satisfactory result. The last step, printing the picture on sensitized paper, was relatively simple.

As a photographer, she was ruthless. Children, her favorite subject, feared her. Julia Margaret lurked by the door, ready to stop a passing child for hours of posing. Edith Bradley Ellison recalled that the children of Freshwater "loved" her but "fled from her." When they saw her, they'd call out, "She's coming! She'll catch one of us!" And when Julia Margaret caught them, she bribed them with candy to pose. Three captives appear in *Blackberry Gathering*. And another trio shows up in a picture titled *Days at Freshwater*.

Her great-nieces Laura and Rachel Gurney came to pose one day when they were visiting their grandmother, Julia Margaret's sister Sara.

Aunt Julia dressed the girls as angels of the Nativity and fastened heavy swan's wings to their shoulders. She posed them like the angels in Raphael's painting *The Sistine Madonna*. She called her photos *Angel of the Nativity* and *I Wait*.

Her great-nieces Laura and Rachel Gurney came to pose one day.

"No wonder those old photographs of us, leaning over our imaginary ramparts of heaven, look anxious and wistful," said Laura. "This is how we felt for we never knew what Aunt Julia was going to do next. . . . Once in her clutches, we were perfectly helpless. 'Stand there!' she shouted, and we stood for hours, gazing at the model of the heavenly babe (in reality a sleeping child)."

Once the American poet William Wadsworth Longfellow, who wrote *The Song of Hiawatha,* came to Freshwater to visit Alfred Tennyson. Tennyson brought Longfellow over to see his next-door neighbor, Julia Margaret. "You will have to do whatever she tells you," Tennyson warned Longfellow. "I will be back soon and see what is left of you." And he strode across the lawn.

Of course, Julia Margaret took pictures of Tennyson, too. One image shows him with a trimmed beard and wearing a beret. In another, his hair springs wildly from his head. Julia Margaret preferred this messy look to express Tennyson's true character. And Tennyson said it was his favorite portrait of himself, although he complained about the bags under his eyes that appeared in every picture. Julia Margaret never retouched a photograph the way commercial photographers did to please their clients' vanity.

Eagerly, she would dash from the darkroom into the house to show off her latest work. "My husband from first to last has watched every picture with delight," she wrote. "It is my daily habit to run to him with every glass upon which a fresh glory is newly stamped, and to listen to his enthusiastic applause."

Julia Margaret's husband was content to read the classics while she worked, and he posed as King Lear or Merlin whenever she told him to. He didn't mind that she dripped chemicals all over the floor and stained the table linen. The house smelled of collodion, the solution she used. Copying frames were spread out on the lawn, and tubs of soaking prints stood everywhere. Her cook and maids were too busy posing and helping in the darkroom to do their regular jobs. Guests complained of waiting for hours for lunch to be served.

One of the maids, Mary Hillier, posed for so many pictures depicting the Madonna that locals named her "the Island Madonna." In a photograph titled *Devotion,* she gazes tenderly at Julia Margaret's baby grandson, Archibald Cameron, fast asleep.

Mary Ryan, another maid who modeled, had been raised by Julia Margaret. When Mary was a little girl, her mother, an Irish beggar, approached Julia Margaret on a street in London. Julia Margaret was struck by the child's beauty and offered to take the two of them home with her. Julia Margaret found work for Mrs. Ryan in London, and she raised Mary at Freshwater with her two youngest sons. When Mary was seventeen, Julia Margaret sent her to London to deliver a batch of photographs. A rich young man admired her and bought all the pictures in which she appeared. A year and a half later, he came to Dimbola and asked for her hand in marriage.

Julia Margaret photographed Mary and her fiancé as Romeo and Juliet.

A month before the wedding, Julia Margaret photographed Mary and her fiancé as Romeo and Juliet. They were married at Dimbola, and Julia Margaret's husband escorted Mary down the aisle.

In April 1864, Julia Margaret exhibited her work for the first time. But her out-of-focus pictures were seen as incompetent. Critics accused her of ignorance and said her soft effects were due to "faulty" technique and "slovenly manipulation." When she submitted a batch of pictures to the Photographic Society in the winter of 1865, she didn't win a prize. A critic wrote, "We must give this lady credit for daring originality, but at the expense of all other photographic qualities." The *British Journal of Photography* said about Julia Margaret, "Never has any photographer been subject to greater criticism than this lady."

Undaunted, Julia Margaret pursued her work. Not only did she want to create beauty, but she also intended to earn money from her art. Photographic supplies cost a great deal, and her husband's coffee plantations in Ceylon were doing poorly. Besides, they had sons attending college and had to pay their tuition.

In 1865, Julia Margaret copyrighted ninety-one photographs, gave albums to important friends and critics, and exhibited wherever she could. In Berlin, Germany, she won a bronze medal at an exhibition, then a gold.

At her sister Sara's home, Little Holland House, she set up her equipment and made portraits of influential people. One of them was Henry Cole, founder of the South Kensington Museum (now the Victoria and Albert). She gave Cole a portfolio of her photographs, hoping he would include some in the new museum. And he did. On August 10, 1865, Cole bought eighty of Julia Margaret's prints. It was her first major sale. In September, she gave him thirty-four more pictures, free of charge.

Now Julia Margaret's work came to the attention of the public. Her pictures were widely displayed. Other museums borrowed her photographs from the South Kensington. With Cole's support, she achieved her goal. Photography was

recognized as "high art." Cole even gave Julia Margaret a studio in the museum.

In November, she had her first one-woman show, at Colnaghi's, a London photography gallery. Customers who bought her prints could choose tones of gray or brown. She wrote on the mats framing the pictures, "From Life. Copyright Registered Photograph. Julia Margaret Cameron." A critic referring to her out-of-focus technique gave her a rave review. He wrote, "Mrs. Cameron was the first person who had the wit to see that her mistakes were her successes."

In 1867, she began a series of life-size heads featuring the geniuses she admired. No one had ever taken pictures like these before. When she brought her equipment to Sir John Herschel's house, she insisted on washing his white hair and fluffing it up to achieve a "halo" effect. She believed that "great thoughts shone like haloes from the heads of great men."

"Great thoughts shone like haloes from the heads of great men."

Her portraits of Victorian notables brought her fame, although the sitters still objected to the long poses. Preserving likenesses of such men as Charles Darwin and Alfred Tennyson while portraying their inner qualities was one of her important achievements. When ordinary people asked her to photograph them, she refused. She selected her sitters carefully. In a letter to a friend, she said that there were three reasons she photographed: "great beauty — great celebrity — and great friendship."

During the eleven years of her career in England, Julia Margaret produced three thousand photographs. In 1875, she and her husband moved to his beloved Ceylon. There, she still photographed occasionally. When a well-known artist, Marianne North, visited them in 1877, Julia Margaret forced the woman to pose in the heat of the noonday sun.

"She dressed me up in flowing draperies," recalled Miss North, "and made me stand with spiky cocoa-nut branches running into my head . . . and told me to look perfectly natural (with the thermometer standing at 96 degrees)!"

"She . . . told me to look perfectly natural (with the thermometer standing at 96 degrees)!"

While visiting the Camerons, Miss North admired Julia Margaret's green shawl, and Julia Margaret promptly cut it in two and gave Miss North half.

Before leaving England, Julia Margaret had begun writing an account of her career in photography: *Annals of My Glass House*. In the memoir, she wrote, "I longed to arrest all beauty that came before me, and at length the longing has been satisfied."

On January 26, 1879, after a bout of bronchitis, Julia Margaret died in Ceylon. She was sixty-three. On her deathbed, she looked out the window at the stars in the evening sky and said her last word:

"Beautiful."

Acknowledgments

I must begin by thanking my editor, Liz Bicknell, for responding immediately to the idea of a book about Julia Margaret Cameron. Her wit and vision shaped this book. A huge thank-you to Bagram Ibatoulline for his superb, exquisite illustrations that bring Cameron's story to life. And thanks to everyone at Candlewick, especially Katie Cunningham and Carter Hasegawa for working closely with me and to Chris Paul and Amy Berniker for the brilliant design of the book.

I am indebted to John Harris, who first suggested introducing young readers to Cameron's work. Most of all I am grateful to Linda Zuckerman for inviting Liz Bicknell and me, one summer, to be on the faculty of the Pacific Northwest Children's Book Conference, where we met.

As always, a bouquet of thanks to my friend and agent, George Nicholson, for his support, and to his assistants, Caitlin McDonald and Erica Rand Silverman. I want to express my appreciation to Julian Cox, chief curator of the de Young Museum, for generously sharing information about Julia Margaret Cameron. Finally, my deepest thanks to my writers' group for their helpful critiques and encouragement, and to my husband, Michael B. Rubin.

Source Notes

p. ix "It is a sacred . . . to very many": Quoted in Hill, pp. 153–154.

p. 1 "the beautiful Miss Pattles": Ibid., p. 15.

p. 1 "a little, ugly, underbred-looking . . . better than beauty": Isabella Fane quoted in Olsen, p. 33.

p. 2 "deeply seated love of the beautiful": Cameron, "Annals of My Glass House," reprinted in Weaver, p. 154.

p. 2 "I longed to arrest . . . came before me": Ibid., p. 155.

p. 5 "young gentleman writer": Hill, p. 23.

p. 12 "dusty lanes": Hill, p. 28.

p. 12 "embodiment of a prayer": Cameron, "Annals," in Weaver, p. 157.

p. 19 "You were my first Teacher . . . were given to me": Quoted in Olsen, p. 49.

p. 20 "Behold the most . . . man on earth!": Ibid., p. 29.

p. 22 "pure joy": Ibid., p. 52.

p. 29 "a strange apparition . . . summer time": Ibid., p. 79.

p. 29 "trailing draperies" and "which she stirred as she walked along": Ibid., p. 80.

p. 30 "cartomania craze": Philippa Wright, "Little Pictures: Julia Margaret Cameron and Small-Format Photography," in Cox and Ford, p. 82.

p. 30 "loses the look of peace!": Quoted in Olsen, p. 102.

p. 32 "It may amuse . . . solitude at Freshwater," "The gift from . . . love of the beautiful," and "living thing": Cameron, "Annals," in Weaver, p. 154.

p. 32 "unassisted": Cameron to John Herschel quoted in Olsen, p. 145.

p. 32 "I began with . . . focus my sitter": Cameron, "Annals," in Weaver, p. 155.

p. 34 "The hens were . . . not eaten": Ibid. and quoted in Olsen, p. 146.

p. 34 "All thro' the . . . endless failures": Cameron to John Herschel quoted in Olsen, p. 145.

p. 34 "first success": Cameron, "Annals," in Weaver, p. 155.

p. 37 "I ran all over . . . for the child": Ibid.

p. 37 "My first perfect . . . little sitter": Quoted in Colin Ford, "Geniuses, Poets, and Painters: The World of Julia Margaret Cameron," in Cox and Ford, p. 24.

p. 37 "I get into difficulties . . . out of them": Cameron to John Herschel quoted in Olsen, p. 149.

p. 38 "My out-of-focus pictures were a fluke": Cameron, "Annals," in Weaver, p. 155, and quoted in Olsen, p. 147.

p. 41 "Why does not . . . shall be made *Immortal*" and "I am Mrs. Cameron . . . let me do so?": Quoted in Gernsheim, p. 32.

p. 41 "ordeal": Ibid., p. 43, and quoted in Hill, p. 109.

p. 41 "We came at . . . turned upon us": Quoted in Gernsheim, p. 30.

p. 43 "was very untidy and very uncomfortable": Quoted in Hill, p. 109.

p. 43　"It was *torture* to sit so long": Wilfred Ward quoted in Gernsheim, p. 30.

p. 43　"Mrs. Cameron put . . . heroic queen" and "A minute went . . . down my forehead": Quoted in Hill, p. 109.

p. 46　"loved," "fled from her," and "She's coming! She'll catch one of us!": Edith Bradley Ellison quoted in Olsen, p. 151.

p. 49　"No wonder those . . . a sleeping child)," "You will have . . . she tells you," and "I will be back . . . left of you": Quoted in Troubridge, p. 34.

p. 50　"My husband from . . . his enthusiastic applause": Cameron, "Annals," in Weaver, p. 155.

p. 53　"faulty": *ET Journal* quoted in Olsen, p. 177.

p. 53　"slovenly manipulation": *The Photographic Journal*, December 1865, quoted in Gernsheim, p. 63.

p. 53　"We must give . . . photographic qualities": *The Photographic Journal* quoted in Hill, p. 127.

p. 53　"Never has any . . . than this lady": *The British Journal of Photography* quoted in Olsen, p. 175.

p. 56　"high art": Hopkinson, p. 161.

p. 56　"From Life . . . Cameron": Hill, p. 126.

p. 56　"Mrs. Cameron was . . . her successes": Coventry Patmore quoted in Olsen, p. 183.

p. 56　"great thoughts . . . of great men": Quoted in Hopkinson, p. 116.

p. 58 "great beauty — great celebrity — and great friendship": Cameron to
William Gregory quoted in Olsen, p. 222.

p. 58 "She dressed me up . . . at 96 degrees)!": Quoted in Hill,
p. 151.

p. 61 "I longed to arrest . . . longing has been satisfied": Cameron, "Annals," in
Weaver, p. 155.

p. 61 "Beautiful": Quoted in Hopkinson, p. 93.

Bibliography

EXHIBIT CATALOG

Howard, Jeremy. *Whisper of the Muse: The World of Julia Margaret Cameron.* London: P & D Colnaghi & Co., 1990.

BOOKS

Cameron, Julia Margaret. *Victorian Photographs of Famous Men & Fair Women.* Edited by Tristram Powell. Boston: Godine, 1973.

Cox, Julian, and Colin Ford. *Julia Margaret Cameron: The Complete Photographs.* Los Angeles: Getty Museum, 2003.

Ford, Colin. *Julia Margaret Cameron: A Critical Biography.* Los Angeles: Getty Museum, 2003.

Gernsheim, Helmut. *Julia Margaret Cameron: Her Life and Photographic Work.* Millerton, NY: Aperture, 1975.

Hill, Brian. *Julia Margaret Cameron: A Victorian Family Portrait.* New York: St. Martin's, 1973.

Hopkinson, Amanda. *Julia Margaret Cameron.* London: Virago, 1986.

Lukitsh, Joanne. *Julia Margaret Cameron.* London: Phaidon, 2001.

Olsen, Victoria C. *From Life: Julia Margaret Cameron and Victorian Photography.* New York: Palgrave Macmillan, 2003.

Troubridge, Laura. *Memories and Reflections.* London: Heinemann, 1925.

Weaver, Mike. *Julia Margaret Cameron: 1815–1879.* Boston: Little, Brown, 1984.

Museums

If you would like to see Julia Margaret Cameron's work,
it can be viewed at the following museums:

UNITED STATES

Art Institute of Chicago • Cantor Arts Center at Stanford University, Palo Alto

de Young Fine Arts Museums of San Francisco

George Eastman House, International Museum
of Photography and Film, Rochester, NY

Harry Ransom Center, University of Texas at Austin

High Museum of Art, Atlanta

J. Paul Getty Museum, Los Angeles • Metropolitan Museum of Art, New York

Museum of Fine Arts, Boston • Museum of Modern Art, New York

University of New Mexico Art Museum, Albuquerque

ENGLAND

Dimbola Museum & Galleries, Isle of Wight

Leighton House Museum, London

National Media Museum, Bradford • National Portrait Gallery, London

Science & Society Picture Library, London

Tennyson Research Centre, Lincoln

Victoria and Albert Museum, London

Photography Credits

p. 3 "Young Girl Praying," 1866, by Julia Margaret Cameron. Albumen silver print. 29.5 x 26 cm (11⅝ x 10¼ in.). Courtesy of the J. Paul Getty Museum, Los Angeles.

p. 7 "Baby Pictet," courtesy of the National Media Museum/Science & Society Picture Library.

p. 13 "Paul and Virginia," 1864, by Julia Margaret Cameron. Albumen silver print. 25.4 x 19.8 cm (10 x 7¹³⁄₁₆ in.). Courtesy of the J. Paul Getty Museum, Los Angeles.

p. 21 "Charles Hay Cameron," 1864, by Julia Margaret Cameron. Albumen silver print. 29.2 x 22.4 cm (11½ x 8¹³⁄₁₆ in.). Courtesy of the J. Paul Getty Museum, Los Angeles.

p. 27 "The Rosebud Garden of Girls," June 1868, by Julia Margaret Cameron. Albumen silver print. 29.4 x 26.7 cm (11⁹⁄₁₆ x 10½ in.). Courtesy of the J. Paul Getty Museum, Los Angeles.

p. 30 "My Son Eugene of the RA," courtesy of the National Media Museum/Science & Society Picture Library.

p. 35 "Annie," January 1864, by Julia Margaret Cameron. Albumen silver print. 17.9 x 14.3 cm (7¹⁄₁₆ x 5⅝ in.). Courtesy of the J. Paul Getty Museum, Los Angeles.

p. 39 "A Study of the Cenci," 1868, by Julia Margaret Cameron. Albumen silver print. 32.7 x 24.6 cm (12⅞ x 9¹¹⁄₁₆ in.). Courtesy of the J. Paul Getty Museum, Los Angeles.

p. 42 "Despair," courtesy of the Royal Photographic Society Collection/ National Media Museum, United Kingdom.

p. 47 "I Wait (Rachel Gurney)," 1872, by Julia Margaret Cameron. Albumen silver print. 32.7 x 25.4 cm (12⅞ x 10 in.). Courtesy of the J. Paul Getty Museum, Los Angeles.

p. 52 "Romeo and Juliet," courtesy of the Harry Ransom Center at the University of Texas at Austin.

p. 57 "J.F.W. Herschel," April 1867, by Julia Margaret Cameron. Albumen silver print. 35.4 x 27.3 cm (13¹⁵⁄₁₆ x 10¾ in.). Courtesy of the J. Paul Getty Museum, Los Angeles.

p. 59 "Marianne North," © Julia Margaret Cameron/Board of Trustees of the Royal Botanic Gardens, Kew.

Index